**Editor**
Stephanie Buehler, M.P.W., M.A.

**Editorial Project Manager**
Ina Massler Levin, M.A.

**Editor in Chief**
Sharon Coan, M.S. Ed.

**Illustrator**
Chandler Sinnott

**Cover Artist**
Sue Fullam

**Art Coordinator**
Denice Adorno

**Creative Director**
Elayne Roberts

**Imaging**
Ralph Olmedo, Jr.

**Product Manager**
Phil Garcia

**Acknowledgements**
*KidPix*® is a registered trademark of The Learning Company.

**Publishers**
Rachelle Cracchiolo, M.S. Ed.
Mary Dupuy Smith, M.S. Ed.

# How to Make a Book Report

## Grades 1–3

**Author**

*Jennifer Overend Prior, M.Ed.*

*Teacher Created Materials, Inc.*
6421 Industry Way
Westminster, CA 92683
www.teachercreated.com
**ISBN-1-57690-503-9**
©*1999 Teacher Created Materials, Inc.*
Reprinted, 2000
Made in U.S.A.

# Table of Contents

# Introduction

You'd never imagine that making a book report could be so exciting. This book will help your children understand the basics of writing book reports, as well as provide creative book-project ideas that they are sure to love. Projects have been separated into categories such as character reports, plot reports, story detail reports, author/illustrator reports, book recommendations, and book presentations. Many of these projects can be completed either in small groups or as entertaining and educational homework assignments. However you choose to use them, the result is sure to be impressive.

This book is divided into the following sections:

## Book Report Basics

This section will help your students get started. It introduces the necessary skills and knowledge children need to create effective book reports, from using proper writing skills to summarizing material. Two class projects are included to help your children understand the process of book reporting.

## Character Reports

Make a pop-up card, write a poem, or dress up as a character. This section is filled with creative ideas for reporting about the characters in a book.

## Plot Reports

This section contains projects for reporting on the specific sequence of events in a story. These activities result in newsletters, child-created books, and more.

## Story Detail Reports

Gameboards, word searches, story maps, and research are all a part of this section. These activities encourage your children to think about the details of a story, from its events to its vocabulary.

## Author/Illustrator Reports

The projects in this section will give your students the opportunity to read and compare books written by different authors. They can also experiment with the artistic styles of popular children's book illustrators.

## Book Recommendations

This section encourages children to tell others about the books they have read. Your students will learn how to make a book advertisement and learn how to rate the elements of their books on a scale.

## Book Presentations

Presenting books to the class doesn't have to be scary. In fact, these projects make book presentations just plain fun. This section contains ideas for planning oral reports, creating puppet shows, and making a multimedia computer presentation. So, what are you waiting for? Let the fun begin!

# So Many Books, So Much Time!

There are many kinds of books. Use this chart to track the books you listen to or read. Each time you read a different kind of book, color in a square on the chart.

| Funny Story | Mystery | Any Kind of Chapter Book | Caldecott Medal Winner | Newbery Medal Winner |
|---|---|---|---|---|
| Nonfiction Story | Animal Story | Tall Tale | Realistic Fiction Story | Legend |
| Steven Kellogg Story | Tomie dePaola Story | Marc Brown Story | Audrey Wood Story | Don Freeman Story |
| Free Choice | Free Choice | Free Choice | Free Choice | Free Choice |

# Writing Skills

The basic steps in the writing process include the following:

## Prewriting

In this step you brainstorm, think about your topic, create webs and clusters, outline, research, and play around with ideas and words.

## First Draft Writing

This is when you simply write all your ideas. Don't worry about anything except saying what you want to say.

## Revision

After you write your rough draft, go back over what you wrote. Correct spelling and grammar, look up any words you need to, take some things out and add others, and arrange your paragraphs.

## Evaluation

Share your work with someone. This person could be your teacher, a friend or parent, a classmate, or others in a writers' workshop. Collect valuable information about what works and what doesn't work in your report.

## Editing and Rewriting

Now that you have some fresh ideas, go over your work again. Correct any spelling or grammatical errors you might have missed before; add any ideas you got from others that you liked. Make a final copy of your writing.

## Publishing

When others are able to read your finished product, you have published. Your work may appear on a bulletin board, in a class book, in your own book, in a portfolio, or in a newsletter.

## Evaluation

In this stage, your teacher or your classmates will let you know what they think of your report. Your teacher will evaluate your report to make sure you completed it according to the directions given to you.

# Writing Skills *(cont.)*

## Basic Book Report Writing Essentials

### For a Fiction Book

**Include the title and author's name**. Don't forget your own name as the author of the book report.

**Compose a theme statement.** This will really impress your teacher. The theme is the main idea of the story. To help you figure out what the theme is in your book, ask yourself these questions:

What does the main character learn by the end of the book? What is the author's purpose in writing the book? Or, if someone asked you to quickly say what the book is about, what would you say?

**Summarize the story.** This is writing about the plot. The summary is different from the theme because in the summary you tell what happens in the story, especially what happens to the main character. Be sure you have a beginning, a middle, and an ending in your summary, just as you would in a story.

**Give your opinion.** End your book report by saying whether or not you liked the book and whether or not you would recommend it to your friends to read.

---

### For a Nonfiction Book

**Include the title, author's name, and your name.**

**Compose a theme statement.** For a nonfiction book it might be, "The author wanted to show that spiders are fascinating and are not to be feared."

**Summarize.** Cover the topics as listed in the table of contents. Give a few details for each, perhaps interesting things you learned.

**State your opinion.** In addition to stating whether or not you liked the book, think about the following: Did the author provide the information you expected to find? Was the writing interesting and easy to understand? Did you learn anything new?

▲▽ ▲▽ ▲▽ ▲▽ ▲▽ ▲▽ ▲▽ ▲▽ ▶

# Summarizing

Summarizing is a not always easy to do. If your family told you to pack a small bag with only your favorite and most important things, could you do it in one minute? Summarizing is like that. A summary includes only the most important things. You can easily figure out the most important things in a story by asking who, what, where, when, why, and how questions. For some books, you may not use all of these. In a summary, you can include:

- *who* the story is about
- *what* happens
- *when* it happens
- *where* it happens
- *why* it happens

Summaries are always short. They can be as short as four or five sentences. Your teacher will tell you how long your summary should be.

Here is a story chart that can help you figure out the most important things in a book you have read. Use the ideas on your completed chart to write your summary.

## Summarizing Chart

| |
|---|
| **Who was the main character?** |
| **Tell about the main character.** |
| **Where did the story take place?** |
| **What was the character's problem?** |
| **How was the problem solved?** |

# Write a Book Report

**Name** _____

**Title of Book** _____

**Author** _____

**Illustrator** _____

**Story Summary**

_____

_____

_____

_____

_____

_____

**Story Illustration**

# Story Journaling

Making a good book report begins with reading a good book. Keep track of the books you read by journaling about them. When you are ready to make a book report, review your story journal to choose a good book.

| Name of Story | Author | This story is about: |
|---|---|---|
|  |  |  |
|  |  |  |
|  |  |  |
|  |  |  |
|  |  |  |
|  |  |  |
|  |  |  |
|  |  |  |
|  |  |  |
|  |  |  |
|  |  |  |

# Class Summary Book

This group activity will help your children to improve their skills in summarizing while enjoying a read-aloud chapter book.

## Day 1

To begin, prepare a table with paint, water, a paintbrush, and a 12" x 18" ( 30 cm x 46 cm) sheet of construction paper. Choose an eventful read-aloud book with several chapters. Before reading the day's new chapter, choose a child to be the artist. While listening to the chapter, this child thinks of an illustration that represents an event in the chapter. He or she may begin to paint the illustration at any time during the reading. Allow the painting to dry.

## Day 2

On the following day, before reading the next chapter, have the child share his or her illustration. Then ask all of the children to summarize the events of the previous day's chapter. Write a brief summary of the chapter on the illustration as the children dictate. Now it's time to choose a new artist for the next chapter. Continue in this manner each day until you have completed reading the book to your class.

## Assembling the Book

Stack the summary/illustration pages in order from beginning to end. Invite a child to paint a cover for the book, including the chapter book's title and author. Allow the cover to dry and then place it atop the stacked pages. You can bind the pages together using loops of yarn, metal shower-curtain rings, or by using a binding machine with a plastic spiral binder.

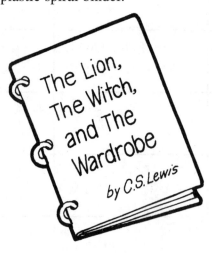

## Displaying the Book

Place the completed summary book in a prominent location and encourage your children to read it in their free time. Exposure to the class-generated summaries will not only allow them to relive the events of the read-aloud book, but it will also help them to better understand the process of summarizing.

# Class Graphs

Give your children the opportunity to express their literary likes and dislikes with class graphing activities they'll really enjoy making.

## Pile 'em Up

For this three-dimensional book graph, you'll need a supply of books (one per child) that are all approximately the same thickness. Read a book to your class. Ask the children to think about the things they liked or disliked about the book and have them each rate the book on the following scale: Great, Okay, and Bad. Designate a place on the floor for each rating category. Then ask each child to stack a book in one of the piles according to his or her rating choice. When all of the books are piled up, ask the children questions about this 3-D graph, such as the following:

- How did most of the children feel about the book?

- Did more children like the book or dislike the book?

- How many children thought the book was okay?

## Clip It On

This graphing activity gives your children the opportunity to compare books. Begin by reading two books to your class. Ask them to think about the story events and characters. Which book was more entertaining? Which book had better illustrations? Create a clothespin graph by dividing a posterboard into two columns. Label the top of each column with the title of one of the books. Then have each child clip a clothespin onto the side labeled with his or her favorite book. Calculate the total number of children who selected each book and encourage them to share the reasons they made their choices.

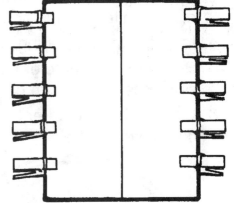

## Author's Best

Present your children with a variety of books written by the same author. Read several of the author's books to your class. Ask each child to choose a favorite book and encourage him or her to think of several reasons why that book is his or her favorite. Create and label an author bar graph as shown. To indicate a favorite book, each child draws a self-portrait on a two-inch (5 cm) construction-paper square and then attaches it in the row beside his or her favorite book.

# Multi-Picture Character Frame

You can display the characters in your story in an attractive picture frame. Here's how:

## Materials

- one 9" x 12" (23 cm x 30 cm) sheet of colored construction paper
- scissors
- glue
- one 9" x 12" (23 cm x 30 cm) sheet of white construction paper
- black marker
- crayons

## Directions

1. Choose three or four characters from the story you read. Make a frame for each.
2. On the colored construction paper, cut a two- or three-inch (5–7.6 cm) shape for each character you have selected. Discard the cutouts.
3. Spread glue on the multi-picture frame you have just created; place it on top of the white construction paper, with the edges aligned.
4. In each frame opening, color a character from the story.
5. Below each character illustration, write the character's name and a few sentences about him or her, using the black marker.
6. Use the black marker to write the title of the book at the top of your completed frame.

# If I Were the Character . . .

If you were the character is this story, how would you feel? What would you do? Complete the sentences below to make a free-verse poem. (It does not have to rhyme.) Read your poem to the class.

**Student's Name:** _____

**Book Title:** _____

**Author:** _____

If I were _____

I would feel_____because _____

_____

I would have_____because _____

_____

If I were_____, I would go_____because_____

_____

I would try_____because _____

_____

If I were_____, I would want _____because _____

_____

But most of all, I would _____

_____

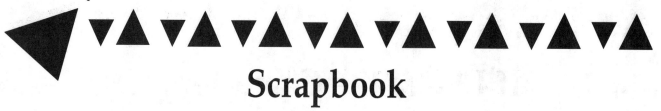

# Scrapbook

You can make a scrapbook about a character in the book you have read. Choose a character in your book and think about the things you know about him or her.

## The Scrapbook

Assemble a scrapbook using a three-ring notebook. Place several sheets of sturdy paper in the notebook. On the first page, write the name of the character and the title and author of the book. On each of the scrapbook pages, glue small objects, figurines, or magazine cutouts that represent something about the character. Beside each object write about how it relates to the character. See the examples below to help you with items to include in your scrapbook.

## Likes and Dislikes

What things did your character like or dislike?

- pets (magazine cutouts, small animal figurine)
- friends (pictures, objects showing things they liked to do together)
- toys (drawings of the toys, game pieces, or dice)
- food (drawings or cutouts)
- school (small school items, such as a pencil, writing paper, or a test paper)

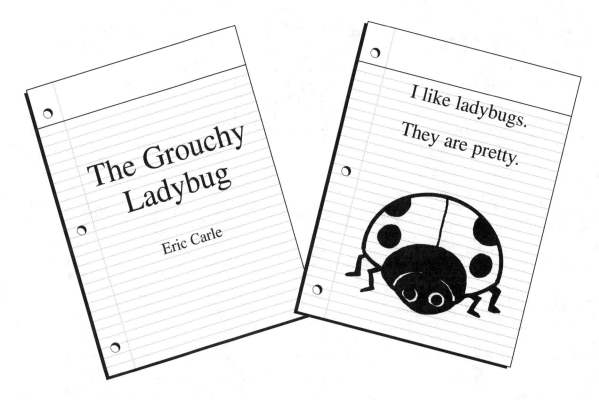

# Scrapbook *(cont.)*

## Family Members

Did your character have family members who were a part of the story? Did he or she have a brother or a sister? How did the character feel about his or her family members?

- gifts given or received (cutouts or figurines)
- activities done together (drawings or cutouts)
- trip taken together (design a postcard showing the trip location)

## Hobbies

Did your character have a hobby or things that he or she liked to do?

- sports (small, plastic, sports ball; magazine cutouts)
- art (small art item, such as a crayon or a paintbrush)

## Events

Where did your character go in the story? What things did your character do?

- movie (actual ticket stubs, or drawings of tickets)
- neighborhood (map showing the neighborhood)
- store (drawing of the store and where the character went in the store)

Be creative! Add as many objects, drawings, and cutouts as you can find. Be sure to write about each one.

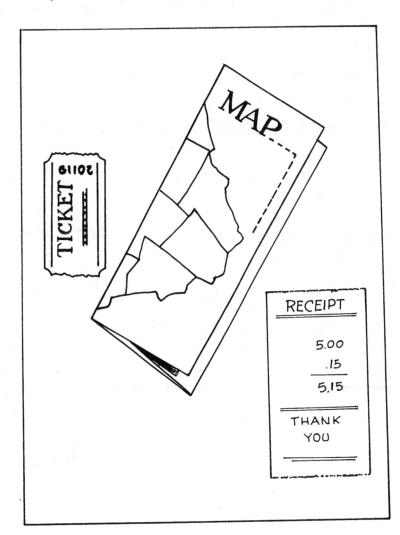

# Character Dress-up

Here is a fun way to tell about a character in a story. Look at the illustrations or read the descriptions of the clothes the character wore.

- Was the character a person or an animal?

- If the character was a person, did he or she wear different outfits, or was he or she wearing the same thing throughout the story?

- Did the character have a special hairstyle?

- Did the character wear glasses?

- Did the character carry anything with him or her, such as a toy, a doll, a ball, or a backpack?

Now think about how you could dress up like this character. Check your closet for clothes that are similar to the character's clothes. Make glasses or a hat out of construction paper.

If your character is an animal, make construction-paper ears, a nose, wings, or a tail. Gather the necessary items that the character carried with him or her.

## The Dress-Up Presentation

On the day you dress up to show your teacher and classmates, pretend you are the character. Introduce yourself and tell the name and author of the book, as well as the events of the story as if they really happened to you as that character. Invite your teacher and classmates to ask questions.

# Character Poems

Writing a character poem is a great way to tell people about a story you have read and the main character in it.  Here are few ideas:

## Cinquain Poem

Line 1: character's name

Line 2: two adjectives describing the character

Line 3: three verbs showing what the character does

Line 4: a sentence or phrase about the character

Line 5: one word to rename the character
(boy, girl, student, friend, etc.)

*Wilbur*
*special, shy*
*sleeps, eats, plays*
*Charlotte's special friend*
*pig*

## List Poem

Line 1: character's name

Line 2: adjective describing the character

Line 3: adjective describing the character

Line 4: adjective describing the character

Line 5: adjective describing the character

Line 6: adjective describing the character

Line 7: adjective describing the character

Line 8: adjective describing the character

*George*
*curious*
*adventurous*
*funny*
*silly*
*quick*
*athletic*
*unique*

## Haiku

Line 1: phrase with five syllables

Line 2: phrase with seven syllables

Line 3: phrase with five syllables

*The cat wears a hat.*
*He tells special stories, too.*
*He creates mischief.*

Choose one of the poems above and, on a separate piece of paper, write your own character poem.

Book Title: _____

Author: _____

Type of poem: _____

# Character Diary

Using a character diary, you can tell about a story by pretending to be a character in it. Practice thinking about the story as if you are the character.

- What is your name?

- How old are you?

- Who are your friends and/or family members?

- What things do you like to do?

- What things bother you?

- What happened to you in the story?

- How did this event make you feel?

When you write in your diary, respond to the questions above. Feel free to write about other events, problems, and situations that happened in the story. In the book below, draw a picture to go along with your diary entry. As you write, be sure to pretend that you are the character.

Student's Name: _____

Book Title: _____

Author: _____

Date: _____

Dear Diary,

_____

_____

_____

_____

_____

_____

_____

▼▲ ▼▲ ▼▲ ▼▲ ▼▲ ▼▲ ▼▲ ▼▲ ▼▲

# Mystery Character

Your children will all enjoy this detective book project. Display an assortment of pictures books featuring different characters (one for each child). Keep the books on display for a week or two and encourage your children to read as many of the books as possible. At this point, assign each book to a child. Then distribute copies of the clue sheet below for each child to complete about his or her character.

Now let the detective work begin! Display all of the books for the children to see. In turn, have the children read their clues to the class. When a child finishes reading his or her clues, allow the class time to guess the identity of the character. Happy sleuthing!

- - - - - - - - - - - - - - - - - - - - - - - - - - - - - - - - - - - - - - - - - - - - - - - - - - - - - - - - - - - - - - - - - - - -

## Clue Sheet

When writing your clues, think about these things:

- how the character looks
- the friends of the character
- the age of the character
- how he or she feels

- where the character lives
- his or her family members
- the kind of character (person or animal)
- what the character likes to do

Clue #1:_____

Clue #2: _____

Clue #3: _____

Clue #4: _____

Clue #5: _____

Allow classmates to guess who your character is.

My character is _____

from the story _____

# Character Similes

Think about the main character in the book you read. How would you describe his or her personality? Was the character kind? Was he or she funny? Was the character a good friend? In the first column of the chart, make a list of the things that describe him or her. Beside each descriptive word, write a simile about the character. Here are some examples:

| Character Description | Simile |
| --- | --- |
| sweet | She was as sweet as a kitty cat. |
| friendly | She was as friendly as a puppy. |
| silly | She was as silly as a monkey. |
| smart | She was as smart as a professor. |

Book Title: _____

Author: _____

Name of character: _____

_____

| Character Description | Simile |
| --- | --- |
| _____ | _____ |
| _____ | _____ |
| _____ | _____ |
| _____ | _____ |
| _____ | _____ |
| _____ | _____ |
| _____ | _____ |
| _____ | _____ |

Tell your classmates about the book and share your similes with them.

▲▼ ▲▼ ▲▼ ▲▼ ▲▼ ▲▼ ▲▼ ▲▼ ▶

# Accordion-Book Summary

This project displays the events of the book you read in an eye-catching way. To begin, write the title of your book below. Then write three sentences to summarize the story. The easiest way to do this is to write one sentence telling about the beginning of the story, one about the middle of the story, and one about the end of the story.

Book Title: _____

Beginning: _____

_____

Middle: _____

_____

End: _____

_____

Follow the directions to make the accordion book.

## Materials

- one 6" x 18" (15 cm x 46 cm) strip of colored construction paper
- one 6" x 18" (15 cm x 46 cm) strip of white construction paper
- glue
- black marker
- crayons

## Directions

1. Glue together the long sides of the construction paper strips and allow the glue to dry.

2. Fold the project accordion-style into four equal sections. In each section, the top white portion is for the illustration and the colored section below it is for the writing.

3. Write the title of the book on the front of the accordion book and draw an illustration above it.

4. Open the book and, on each of the next three pages, write one of your summary sentences and a picture to go with it.

# A Lesson Learned

Many books teach lessons that can help us in our daily lives.  Think about the book you read.  What lessons did you learn?  Did the main character help you learn the lesson?  Did one of the other characters teach you a lesson?

Book Title: _____

Which character taught you a lesson? _____

What did the character do?

_____

_____

_____

_____

What did you learn?

_____

_____

_____

_____

If something like this happens to you, explain what you will do.

_____

_____

_____

_____

_____

_____

_____

_____

▲▼ ▲▼ ▲▼ ▲▼ ▲▼ ▲▼ ▲▼ ▲▼ ◀

# Become a Reporter

An eye-catching newsletter is a great way to tell about a story you have read. You can write a news report about the main character and events that happened in the story, then add colorful graphics or illustrations. Using the reproducible newsletter on page 24, your final articles and illustrations will look professional.

## The Five Ws

Remember the five Ws when writing a news article: Who? What? Where? When? Why? Be sure to think about the characters, the things they did, where the story took place, when the story happened, and why the events took place.

## Character Article

Write the name and gender of the main character. Write about the character's personality traits. Tell where the story took place and explain the problem the main character encountered in the story. Finally, explain how the character's problem was solved and any other details about the end of the story.

## Event Article

This kind of article can be used to share your favorite part of the story. As you are writing, be sure to explain the events leading up to this event. Describe the setting and other characters who were involved.

## Samples

The book *The Legend of the Bluebonnet* by Tomie dePaola was used to create the following articles for a newsletter:

### Character Article

*She-Who-Is-Alone is a Native American girl. Her family died in a drought and famine. The Comanche people took care of her. She had a doll that was very precious to her. She-Who-Is-Alone sacrificed her doll to save her people.*

### Event Article

*Rain has not fallen in the land for a long time. The Comanche people have very little food and water. The buffalo and the plants are all dying. Many people have died because of the drought and famine. The Comanche people have been praying to the Great Spirits to help them.*

# Newsletter Outline

Title

▲▼ ▲▼ ▲▼ ▲▼ ▲▼ ▲▼ ▲▼ ▲▼ ▶

# What's in the Bag?

This project results in a guessing game for your classmates. Choose a book for your project. Select an important object that is found in the story and place a small replica or picture of the object in a paper lunch sack. For example, using the book *Cloudy with a Chance of Meatballs* by Judi Barrett, you might choose a type of food. For the book *The Legend of the Indian Paintbrush* by Tomie dePaola, you might choose the buckskin canvas.

On the outside of the bag, glue clue cards relating to the object inside. Using the example of *Cloudy with a Chance of Meatballs,* you could place a plastic hot dog inside. Clues on the outside of the bag could be:

- It's something to eat.
- It goes on a bun.
- It's long and skinny.
- Some people like it with mustard.

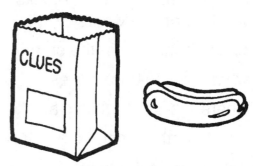

What is it?_____

Read the clues to your classmates and have them guess the identity of the object inside. Then explain why you chose that object and tell a summary of the story.

Brainstorm a list of clues below. Be sure not to make your clues too easy!

Name of book: _____

Author: _____

Clues: _____

_____

_____

_____

What is it?  It's a _____

_____

# Story Gameboard

Making a gameboard is a fun way to show how much you remember about the book you read. It is also a great way to encourage your classmates to read it.

## Question Cards

On each of several 3" x 2" (7.6 cm x 5 cm) cards, write a question about the story. On the back of each card, write the answer to the question. Read the ideas below to help you write the questions.

- main character's feelings
- how the main character looks or what he or she wears
- other characters in the story
- where the character lives
- where the story takes place
- events that happen in the story
- a problem in the story
- how the problem was solved

## The Gameboard and Playing Pieces

Use the pattern on page 27 to design a gameboard for your story. Write the title and author of the book at the top of the gameboard. Color scenes from the story in the spaces. If possible, have an adult laminate the gameboard and question cards. Choose small objects for game pieces, such as pennies or plastic chips.

## Playing the Game

In order to play, your classmates must first read the book. Place the gameboard on a flat surface and stack the question cards face up on the board. Follow the directions on the gameboard to play. The first player to reach "Finish" is the winner.

# Story Gameboard *(cont.)*

_____

Book Title

_____

Author

**Start**

**Finish**

**Card Stack**

1. Player 1 reads the top card in the stack and answers the question.

2. If correct, he or she moves ahead one space. If incorrect, Player 1 does not move ahead.

3. Now, it's Player 2's turn.

4. The first player to reach "Finish" is the winner.

# Make a Word Search

This project involves looking for interesting words the author used in his or her story. Read the story again slowly and carefully. Write interesting or unfamiliar words from the story on the lines below.

Next, use a dictionary to find out the meaning of each word. Write each definition beside the word. Then write a sentence of your own using that word.

Make a word search puzzle using the pattern on page 29. Write the words in the puzzle. Then fill in the remaining boxes of the puzzle with random letters. Be sure to write each word used and its definition on the lines below the puzzle.

Word _____

Definition(s) _____

Sentence(s) _____

Word _____

Definition(s) _____

Sentence(s) _____

Word _____

Definition(s) _____

Sentence(s) _____

Word _____

Definition(s) _____

Sentence(s) _____

# Make a Word Search *(cont.)*

Read each word and its definition.  Find each word in the puzzle and circle it.

|  |  |  |  |  |  |  |
|--|--|--|--|--|--|--|
|  |  |  |  |  |  |  |
|  |  |  |  |  |  |  |
|  |  |  |  |  |  |  |
|  |  |  |  |  |  |  |
|  |  |  |  |  |  |  |

**Words**                                   **Definitions**

_____          _____

_____          _____

_____          _____

_____          _____

_____          _____

_____          _____

_____          _____

# Interesting Words

Demonstrate your knowledge of new vocabulary with this artistic book project. As you read the book, make a list of the interesting or unfamiliar words you find. Use a dictionary to find the meaning of each word and write down the definition. Then, on a large sheet of white construction paper, write each word in a way that represents the meaning of the word as it is used in the story. Use crayons or markers to decoratively write each word. Be creative.

**Book Title:** _____

| **Words** | **Definitions** |
|---|---|
| 1. _____ | _____ |
| 2. _____ | _____ |
| 3. _____ | _____ |
| 4. _____ | _____ |
| 5. _____ | _____ |
| 6. _____ | _____ |
| 7. _____ | _____ |
| 8. _____ | _____ |

Frightening CUTE

# Story Map Poster

How much do you remember about the story you read? This decorative poster will help you show all that you know.

## Materials

- one sheet of lined writing paper
- assorted colors of construction paper
- one large sheet of posterboard or tagboard

- pencil
- black marker
- scissors
- glue

## Directions

1. Make a list of sentences telling about characters and events in the story you read.

2. Cut out 3" shapes from colored construction paper for each sentence that you wrote.

3. Using the black marker, write each sentence neatly on a shape.

4. Arrange the shapes on the posterboard or tagboard in the order that they happened in the story. (Leave space at the top of the poster for the book title.) Arrange the shapes so that they are about 2" apart and glue them in place.

5. Use the black marker to draw an arrow between the shapes. This will guide the reader's eye to each event in the correct sequence.

6. Complete the project by writing the title of the book in large letters at the top of the poster.

MRS. RABBIT SENT THE CHILDREN TO PLAY

PETER ATE TOO MUCH AND GOT SICK

HE RAN AWAY FROM MR. McGREGOR

# Time for a Quiz

You can show your knowledge of a book by making a quiz for future readers of that book. Post your quiz near a displayed copy of the book. After a classmate reads it, he or she can take your quiz to test his or her knowledge of the story.

Use this form to help you create quiz questions.

Write a question about the main character.

_____

Write a question about the main character's personality.

_____

Write a question about the setting of the story.

_____

Write a question about a different character in the story.

_____

Write a question about where the story happened.

_____

Write a question about a problem that happened.

_____

Write a question about an event that happened in the story.

_____

Write a question about how the problem was solved.

_____

# Subject Research

Many books have interesting subjects featured in them. *The Girl Who Loved Wild Horses* by Paul Goble features Native American culture. *Arthur Meets the President* by Marc Brown features the subject of government. If your book features an interesting subject, you can research to find out more information. Here's how to do it:

1. Ask your teacher, librarian, or one of your parents to help you find library books about your subject.

2. Check out books from the library and take several days to read them and look at the pictures.

3. As you find interesting facts about your subject, write them down on the lines below.

4. Draw a picture in the box to show something you learned.

5. Do you still have questions about your subject? Make a list of your questions and try to find the answers by doing more research or by asking an adult.

6. Share the information with your classmates.

**Subject:** _____

**Fact #1:** _____

**Fact #2:** _____

**Fact #3:** _____

**Fact #4:** _____

**My Questions:** _____

_____

# Comparing Books

Many authors have several books they have written. Pages 34 and 35 contain lists of books by popular authors. Choose an author and read several of his or her books. Then use page 36 to write your comparisons.

## Books for Grades 1 and 2

**Don Freeman**

*Bearymore*

*Corduroy*

*Dandelion*

*A Pocket for Corduroy*

*A Rainbow of My Own*

**Steven Kellogg**

*Best Friends*

*Can I Keep Him?*

*Island of the Skog*

*The Mysterious Tadpole*

*Pinkerton, Behave!*

**Arnold Lobel**

*Frog and Toad are Friends*

*Ming Lo Moves the Mountain*

*Mouse Soup*

*On Market Street*

*Owl at Home*

*Uncle Elephant*

**Robert Munsch**

*Angela's Airplane*

*David's Father*

*The Fire Station*

*Love You Forever*

**Robert Munsch** *(cont.)*

*Moira's Birthday*

*Mortimer*

*Paper Bag Princess*

**Marjorie Weinman Sharmat**

*A Big Fat Enormous Lie*

*Gila Monsters Meet You at the Airport*

*Nate the Great*

*Scarlet Monster Lives Here*

**Judith Viorst**

*Alexander and the Terrible, Horrible, No Good, Very Bad Day*

*Alexander, Who Used to be Rich Last Sunday*

*I'll Fix Anthony*

*Rosie and Michael*

*The Tenth Good Thing About Barney*

**Audrey Wood**

*Elbert's Bad Word*

*Heckedy Peg*

*King Bidgood's in the Bathtub*

*Little Penguin's Tale*

*Moonflute*

*The Napping House*

*Quick as a Cricket*

# Comparing Books (cont.)

## Books for Grades 2 and 3

**Byrd Baylor**

*Everybody Needs a Rock*

*Hawk, I'm Your Brother*

*I'm in Charge of Celebrations*

*The Other Way to Listen*

*The Way to Start a Day*

**Paul Goble**

*Beyond the Ridge*

*Crow Chief: A Plains Indian Story*

*Dream Wolf*

*The Gift of the Sacred Dog*

*The Girl Who Loved Wild Horses*

*Iktomi and the Boulder*

**Patricia MacLachlan**

*Arthur for the Very First Time*

*Sarah, Plain and Tall*

*Seven Kisses in a Row*

*Three Names*

*Through Grandpa's Eyes*

**Bill Peet**

*The Ant and the Elephant*

*Big Bad Bruce*

*The Caboose Who Got Loose*

*Eli*

*Farewell to Shady Glade*

**Bill Peet** *(cont.)*

*Kermit the Hermit*

*Randy's Dandy Lions*

*Whingdingdilly*

*The Wump World*

**Patricia Polacco**

*Babushka Baba Yaga*

*Chicken Sunday*

*Keeping Quilt*

*Mrs. Katz and Tush*

*Pink and Say*

*Rechenka's Eggs*

*The Trees of the Dancing Goats*

**Cynthia Rylant**

*Henry and Mudge: The First Book of Their Adventures*

*Missing May*

*Mr. Grigg's Work*

*The Relatives Came*

*When I Was Young in the Mountains*

**Chris Van Allsburg**

*The Garden of Abdul Gasazi*

*Jumanji*

*Just a Dream*

*The Stranger*

*The Wreck of the Zephyr*

# Comparing Books (*cont.*)

The books I read were written by _____

Title of book 1: _____

Title of book 2: _____

Title of book 3: _____

Here's how the books were alike:

_____

_____

_____

_____

Here's how the books were different:

_____

_____

_____

_____

My favorite book was _____

because _____

_____

_____

_____

_____

I would like to read more books by this author:     Yes     No

▲▼ ▲▼ ▲▼ ▲▼ ▲▼ ▲▼ ▲▼ ▲▶

# Works of Art

Many authors create their own illustrations for their books. Choose one of the author/illustrators on pages 37 and 38 to make an artistic book project.

## Ezra Jack Keats

Ezra Jack Keats has a unique artistic style. He combines drawings with collage. Read several of his books (see the list below) and notice his use of paint combined with cutouts of fabric, newspaper, and other materials. Make an illustration of your own to show your favorite part of an Ezra Jack Keats book.

### Materials

- one light-colored sheet of construction paper
- paint and paintbrushes or markers
- assorted colors of paper scraps
- wallpaper scraps
- newspaper
- magazines
- scissors
- glue

### Directions

Draw and colorize your illustration and allow it to dry. Add details to the illustration, such as pictures in frames, clothing, curtains, or furniture, using paper and wallpaper scraps, newspapers, and magazine cutouts.

### Books by Ezra Jack Keats

| | | |
|---|---|---|
| *Apt. 3* | *Jennie's Hat* | *The Snowy Day* |
| *Dreams* | *A Letter to Amy* | *Whistle for Willie* |
| *Goggles* | *Peter's Chair* | |
| *Hi, Cat!* | *Pet Show* | |

## Tomie dePaola

Tomie dePaola's illustrations are clear and simple. Read several of his books (see the list on page 38) and notice his attractive use of colors, simple drawings of people and animals and dark outlines. To make an illustration in this style, use a pencil to draw the picture. Then trace over the pencil lines with a permanent black, fine-tip marker. Add color to the illustration by painting with watercolors.

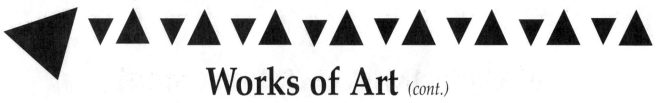

# Works of Art *(cont.)*

## Books by Tomie dePaola

*Art Lesson*

*Bill and Pete*

*Charlie Needs a Cloak*

*The Legend of the Indian Paintbrush*

*Nana Upstairs, Nana Downstairs*

*Now One Foot, Now the Other*

*Strega Nona*

*Strega Nona: Her Story*

## Eric Carle

Look closely at many of Eric Carle's illustrations and you will see a collage of brightly colored tissue paper. Read several of his books (see the list below) and notice the texture (feel) of his illustrations. Some of his illustrations look transparent or see-through. You can make an illustration in this style, too.

## Materials

- one sheet of white construction paper
- pencil
- assorted colors of tissue paper cut into one-inch squares

- diluted glue
- paintbrush
- black marker

## Directions

Draw a large picture on the construction paper using a pencil. (The picture should not be detailed.) Brush the diluted glue onto the picture. Gently place tissue-paper squares onto the glue and press down. Brush on more glue as needed. Be sure to overlap different colors of tissue paper to make interesting color combinations. Allow the illustration to dry overnight; then use the black marker to outline the illustration and to add details.

## Books by Eric Carle

*The Grouchy Ladybug*

*A House for Hermit Crab*

*The Mixed-Up Chameleon*

*Papa, Please Get the Moon for Me*

*Rooster's Off to See the World*

*The Very Hungry Caterpillar*

# Make a Book Advertisement

Advertisers use words and pictures to interest people in their products. You can do the same to interest your classmates in a story you have read. Begin by choosing a book that you really liked.

## Materials

- black marker
- posterboard or sheet of 12" x 18" (30 cm x 46 cm) construction paper scissors
- magazines and newspapers
- glue

## Directions

Using a black marker, write in large letters the title and author of your book at the top of a large sheet of construction paper or posterboard.

Cut out words and phrases from magazines and newspapers that describe your story.

Glue the cutouts, creatively, below the title and author.

At the bottom of the advertisement, write about why this book should be read by your classmates.

# Using a Rating Scale

Tell your classmates about the different parts of your story by using a rating scale. For each rating, explain why you feel this way.

1 = poor
2 = not very good
3 = all right
4 = pretty good
5 = great

---

Write the name of the book below.

_____

How much did you like the main character?                Rating: _____

_____

_____

How much did you like the events in the story?          Rating: _____

_____

_____

How interesting was the story?                          Rating: _____

_____

_____

How funny was the story?                                Rating: _____

_____

_____

How much did you like the illustrations?                Rating: _____

_____

_____

Rate the overall story.                                 Rating: _____

_____

_____

Would you recommend this book to a friend?  Why or why not?

_____

---

▲▼ ▲▼ ▲▼ ▲▼ ▲▼ ▲▼ ▲▼ ▲▼ ▶

# Planning an Oral Report

Presenting an oral report can be a little bit scary, but this planning sheet will help make it easier for you. Rehearse your oral report many times. When presenting, try to use this page as a guide rather than reading from it.

My name is _____

The book I read was _____

It was written by _____

It was illustrated by _____

The book was about (talk about the characters) _____

_____

_____

_____

In the story (talk about the events in the story) _____

_____

_____

_____

My favorite part was when _____

_____

_____

_____

You should read this book because _____

_____

_____

_____

Are there any questions?

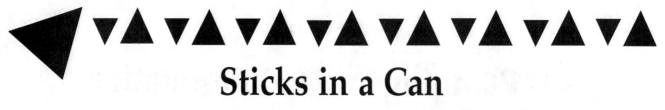

# Sticks in a Can

This book project presentation allows you to show your classmates just how much you know about the book you read.

## Materials

- empty juice can (rinsed)
- decorative adhesive paper
- scissors
- colored permanent markers
- wooden craft sticks
- black fine-tip marker

## Directions

1. Cut a strip of adhesive paper to wrap around the juice can.

2. Use the permanent markers to decorate the outside of the can with the title and author of your book as well as other decorations related to the story.

3. On each of several craft sticks, use a fine-tip marker to write a character name, a name of a location, or an object from the book you read.

4. Place the sticks into the can so that the writing cannot be seen.

5. For your presentation, ask each of your classmates to pass the can and, in turn, select a craft stick.

6. Ask each classmate to read the words on the craft stick to the class.

7. Now it's your turn to explain how this character, location, or object relates to the story you read.

8. When you have explained the words on all of the craft sticks, be sure to invite your classmates to ask questions they have about the story.

▲▼ ▲▼ ▲▼ ▲▼ ▲▼ ▲▼ ▲▼ ▲▼ ▶

# Create a SlideShow Presentation

Teacher Note: This SlideShow presentation has been created, using *Kid Pix 2*®. These instructions can be adapted for use with similar paint programs.

## *Kid Pix 2* Basics

### Getting Started

To begin, click to open *Kid Pix 2*. A drawing screen will appear with a menu bar across the top, a tool bar on the left side, and an options bar below.

### Menus

The **File** menu gives you the opportunity to create New documents, Open existing documents, and Close documents. This menu also allows you to Save, Save As, Print, and Quit.

The **Edit** menu allows you to Undo unwanted actions. It also allows you to Cut, Copy, Paste, and Clear sections of a document.

The **Goodies** menu has many selections. The Small Kids Mode lets you protect your computer programs by keeping young children from straying out of *Kid Pix 2*. The Goodies menu also allows you to Edit Stamps, add letters and symbols to the Wacky Brush alphabet line with Alphabet Text, and Type Text. Additional selections in this menu include Tool Sounds, Record Sound, and Play Sound.

The **Switcheroo** menu gives you the opportunity to Swap Stamps and Swap Hidden Pictures. This menu also has features to explore such as DrawMe. You may also Switch to SlideShow.

### Tool Bar

The tool definitions below are listed in the order in which they appear on the tool bar.

- The Wacky Pencil allows you to draw free-form lines.

- The Line tool allows you to draw straight lines.

- The Rectangle tool creates squares and rectangles in various sizes.

- The Oval tool creates ovals in various sizes.

- The Wacky Brush allows you to paint in a variety of ways.

- The Electric Mixer changes your drawing in many silly ways.

- The Paint Can fills a shape with a selected color or pattern.

- The Eraser allows you to erase part of your picture in the standard way or in some interesting ways.

# Create a SlideShow Presentation *(cont.)*

## *Kid Pix 2* Basics *(cont.)*

### Tool Bar *(cont.)*

- The Text tool places letters, numbers, and symbols on the page.

- The Rubber Stamp tool "stamps" pictures on the screen.

- The Moving Van tool moves a portion of your picture from one place to another.

- The Undo Guy immediately removes the last action performed on the screen. This is a very helpful tool!

- The Color Palette allows you to select colors for drawing, painting, and text.

## Options Bars

Each tool has at least one, if not several, options bars which appear below the Drawing screen. Simply click on a tool in the tool bar and then click on a selection in the options bar. To access more options, click on the arrow at the right end of the bar.

## Putting It All Together

## Create the Slide Show Pages

Think about the book you have read. You will want to make illustrations that represent events in the story. Begin drawing your picture using the following directions:

1. Select the pencil tool and the desired color from the tool bar.

2. In addition to the pencil, you may want to use the paintbrush in creating your picture. Select the paintbrush from the tool bar and the select a painting style from the options bar below it. Any procedure can be removed by immediately selecting the Undo Guy from the tool bar.

3. To add text to the picture, select Type Text from the **Goodies** menu. Click on the screen to place the cursor in the desired location. From the tool bar, select the desired text color. Then type a sentence or two to accompany the picture. If more than one line is needed for the text, it is necessary to press the Return key on the keyboard. Unlike a typical word processing document, the text will not automatically shift to the next line. If you should happen to type beyond the screen, simply press the Delete key on the keyboard until the cursor can be seen again; then press the Return key to move to the next line.

4. Go to the **File** menu and Save the document. Then select Print from the **File** menu.

# Create a SlideShow Presentation *(cont.)*

## *Kid Pix 2* **Basics** *(cont.)*

### How to Create the SlideShow

1. Open SlideShow from the main menu of *Kid Pix 2*.

2. A page of trucks will appear on the screen. Click the small icon of the slide at the base of the first truck. This will bring up a small screen asking which picture you want as the first slide in the slide show.

3. Navigate to and double-click on the desired picture. A thumbnail version of the picture will appear on the truck.

4. On the remaining trucks (or on as many as you choose to use), continue selecting pictures in the same manner for the show.

5. Add sounds to each of the pictures by clicking on the music note on each truck. A menu of sounds will appear. You may preview the sounds before selecting the one you want.

6. Add transitions between the pictures in your slide show by clicking on the Transition box. A menu of transitions will appear. You may preview the transitions before selecting the one you want.

7. Play the SlideShow by clicking on the arrow button at the bottom of the SlideShow screen.

8. Loop the slides to be played over and over together by clicking on the Loop button at the bottom of the SlideShow Screen. To end the slide show, simply double click the mouse or press the Command and Period keys on the keyboard simultaneously.

9. Notice the Undo Guy at the bottom of the screen. Any operation can be removed by clicking this button immediately after the mistake is made.

10. Also notice the stick of dynamite at the bottom of the screen. If at anytime during production you are dissatisfied with the slide show you have created, simply click on this button to erase the show. This will not erase the original pictures, just their usage in the SlideShow.

11. Save the SlideShow using the **File** menu.

# Book-Project Evaluation

Use this form to evaluate a classmate's (or your own) book project.

Evaluator's name _____

Project creator's name _____

What is the title of the book featured in this project?  Who wrote it?

_____

Describe the project.

_____

_____

_____

_____

What did you like about the project?

_____

_____

_____

_____

What did you learn from the project?

_____

_____

_____

_____

Do you plan to read the book?  (Circle one.)        Yes            No

Tell why or why not. _____

_____

_____

# References

**Barrett, Judi**.

*Cloudy with a Chance of Meatballs*. Aladdin Books, 1982.

**Baylor, Byrd**.

*Everybody Needs a Rock*. Aladdin Books, 1987.

*Hawk, I'm Your Brother*. Aladdin Books, 1986.

*I'm in Charge of Celebrations*. Atheneum, 1986.

*The Other Way to Listen*. Alabama Department of Economic, 1997.

*The Way to Start a Day*. Aladdin Books, 1986.

**Carle, Eric**.

*The Grouchy Ladybug*. HarperCollins, 1996.

*A House for Hermit Crab*. Simon & Schuster, 1991.

*The Mixed-Up Chameleon*. HarperCollins, 1988.

*Papa, Please Get the Moon for Me*. Simon & Schuster, 1991.

*Rooster's Off to See the World*. Simon & Schuster, 1992.

*The Very Hungry Caterpillar*. Putnam, 1984.

**dePaola, Tomie**.

*The Art Lesson*. Paperstar, 1997.

*Bill and Pete*. Paperstar, 1996.

*Charlie Needs a Cloak*. Aladdin Books, 1988.

*The Legend of the Bluebonnet*. Putnam, 1986.

*The Legend of the Indian Paintbrush*. Paperstar, 1996.

*Nana Upstairs and Nana Downstairs*. Putnam, 1978.

*Now One Foot, Now the Other*. Putnam, 1988

*Strega Nona: Her Story*. Putnam, 1996.

**Freeman, Don**.

*Bearymore*. Puffin, 1979.

*Corduroy*. Viking Press, 1976.

*Dandelion*. Puffin, 1987.

*A Pocket for Corduroy*. Viking Press, 1997.

*A Rainbow of My Own*. Viking Press, 1978.

**Goble, Paul**.

*Beyond the Ridge*. Aladdin Books, 1993.

*Crow Chief: A Plains Indian Story*. Orchard Books, 1996.

*Dream Wolf*. Aladdin Books, 1997.

*The Gift of the Sacred Dog*. Aladdin Books, 1984.

*The Girl Who Loved Wild Horses*. Simon & Schuster, 1993.

*Iktomi and the Boulder*. Demco Media, 1991.

**Keats, Ezra Jack**.

*Apt. 3*. Aladdin Books, 1986.

*Dreams*. Aladdin Books, 1992.

*Hi, Cat!* Live Oak Media, 1990.

*Jennie's Hat*. HarperCollins, 1985.

*A Letter to Amy*. Puffin, 1998.

*Peter's Chair*. Viking Children's Books, 1998.

*Pet Show*. Aladdin Books, 1987,

*The Snowy Day*. Viking Children's Books, 1996.

*Whistle for Willie*. Viking Children's Books, 1998.

**Kellogg, Steven**.

*Best Friends*. Dial Books, 1992.

*Can I Keep Him?* Dial Books, 1992.

*Island of the Skog*. Dial Books, 1974.

*The Mysterious Tadpole*. Demco Media, 1993.

*Pinkerton, Behave!* Dial Books, 1993.

**Lobel, Arnold**.

*Frog and Toad Are Friends*. HarperCollins, 1979.

*Ming Lo Moves the Mountain*. Mulberry, 1993.

*Mouse Soup*. HarperCollins, 1977.

*On Market Street*. Greenwillow, 1987.

*Owl at Home*. HarperTrophy, 1982.

*Uncle Elephant*. HarperCollins, 1987.

# References (cont.)

**MacLachlan, Patricia.**

*Arthur, for the Very First Time*. HarperTrophy, 1989.

*Sarah, Plain and Tall*. HarperTrophy, 1987.

*Seven Kisses in a Row*. HarperTrophy, 1988.

*Three Names*. HarperCollins, 1991.

*Through Grandpa's Eyes*. HarperCollins, 1994.

**Munsch, Robert.**

*Angela's Airplane*. Demco Media, 1988.

*David's Father*. Firefly Books, 1983.

*The Fire Station*. Annick Press, 1991.

*Love You Forever*. Firefly Books, 1989.

*Moira's Birthday*. Demco Media, 1987.

*Mortimer*. Firefly Books, 1985.

*Paper Bag Princess*. Annick Press, 1988.

**Mayer, Mercer**.

*There's a Nightmare in my Closet*. Dutton, 1992.

**Palacco, Patricia.**

*Babushka Baba Yaga*. Philomel, 1993.

*Chicken Sunday*. Philomel, 1992.

*Keeping Quilt*. Silver Burdett & Ginn, 1993.

*Mrs. Katz and Tush*. Demco Media, 1994.

*Pink and Say*. Philomel, 1994.

*Rechenka's Eggs*. Putnam, 1988.

*The Trees of the Dancing Goats*. Simon & Schuster, 1996.

**Peet, Bill.**

*The Ant and the Elephant*. Sandpiper, 1980.

*Big Bad Bruce*. Houghton Mifflin, 1977.

*Eli*. Houghton Mifflin, 1984.

*Farewell to Shady Glade*. Demco Media, 1981.

*Kermit the Hermit*. Houghton Mifflin, 1980.

*Randy's Dandy Lions*. Houghton Mifflin, 1979.

*The Wump World*. Demco Media, 1981.

**Rylant, Cynthia.**

*Henry and Mudge: The First Book of Their Adventures*. Demco Media, 1990.

*Missing May*. Yearling, 1993.

*Mr. Grigg's Work*. Orchard Books, 1993.

*The Relatives Came*. Demco Media, 1993.

*When I Was Young in the Mountains*. Dutton, 1992.

**Sharmat, Marjorie Weinman.**

*A Big Fat Enormous Lie*. Dutton, 1993.

*Gila Monsters Meet You at the Airport*. Simon & Schuster, 1983.

*Nate the Great*. Young Yearling, 1977.

*Scarlet Monster Lives Here*. HarperTrophy, 1986.

**Van Allsburg, Chris.**

*The Garden of Abdul Gasazi*. Houghton Mifflin, 1994.

*Jumanji*. Scholastic, 1995.

*Just a Dream*. Houghton Mifflin, 1990.

*The Stranger*. Houghton Mifflin, 1986.

*The Wreck of the Zephyr*. Houghton Mifflin, 1983.

**Viorst, Judith.**

*Alexander and the Terrible, Horrible, No Good Very Bad Day*. Atheneum, 1972.

*Alexander, Who Used to Be Rich Last Sunday*. Atheneum, 1978.

*I'll Fix Anthony*. Aladdin Books, 1988.

*Rosie and Michael*. Atheneum, 1974.

*The Tenth Good Thing About Barney*. Atheneum, 1971.

**Wood, Audrey.**

*Elbert's Bad Word*. Harcourt Brace, 1996.

*Heckedy Peg*. Harcourt Brace, 1987.

*King Bidgood's in the Bathtub*. Harcourt Brace, 1985.

*Little Penguin's Tale*. Harcourt Brace, 1993.

*Moonflute*. Harcourt Brace, 1986.

*The Napping House*. Red Wagon, 1996.

*Quick as a Cricket*. Child's Play International, 1996.